new light design

daab

New Light Design es una recopilación de proyectos de iluminación de interiores firmados por algunos de los diseñadores más reconocidos. Se trata de espacios en los que la luz es un elemento tan importante como el mobiliario o la distribución, y en los que se trata este recurso de forma novedosa para que imprima un carácter especial. En este libro la luz trasciende la simple función de iluminar; se convierte en una herramienta con la que resaltar elementos que modifican el espacio y hacen de él algo diferente, que pueden causar un efecto interesante o que simplemente nos gustan. El resultado son viviendas con un sello de identidad propio y original.

New Light Design est un recueil de projets d'éclairage d'intérieurs qui portent la signature des plus grands noms de designers dans ce domaine. La lumière y est considérée comme un élément innovateur, imprégnant l'espace d'originalité, à l'instar du mobilier ou de la distribution spatiale. Dans cet ouvrage, la lumière dépasse sa simple fonction d'éclairage. Elle devient l'instrument qui permet de mettre en valeur les éléments qui sculptent l'espace et le transforment. En les modelant, la lumière crée un effet intéressant ou tout simplement agréable à nos yeux, engendrant des lieux de vie uniques, imprimés du sceau de l'originalité.

New Light Design è una raccolta di progetti di illuminazione di interni firmati da alcuni dei più consolidati light designer del settore. Si tratta di progetti dal carattere speciale e realizzati in maniera innovativa, dove la luce è un elemento così importante come l'arredamento o la distribuzione dello spazio. In questo libro la luce trascende la sua semplice funzione –quella di illuminare–, trasformandosi in uno strumento con cui far risaltare elementi che modificano lo spazio, che possono causare un particolare effetto o che semplicemente sono di nostro gradimento. Il risultato sono delle abitazioni dotate di un marchio di identità proprio ed originale.

New Light Design ist eine Sammlung von Beleuchtungsprojekten im Innenraum, umgesetzt von einigen der innovativsten Designern in diesem Bereich. Dabei handelt es sich um Projekte, bei denen die Beleuchtung ein ebenso entscheidendes Element ist, wie das Mobiliar oder die Aufteilung des Raumes. Dieses Buch liefert neue Lösungsansätze mit einem ganz speziellen Charakter, bei denen das Licht nicht nur zur einfachen Beleuchtung dient, sondern sich in ein Werkzeug verwandelt, mit dem Elemente im Raum hervorgehoben werden können, interessante Effekte erzielt werden oder eine angenehme Atmosphäre geschaffen wird. Damit wird der Gesamteindruck des Wohnraums verändert und bekommt so seine eigene Identität.

New Light Design is a collection of interior lighting projects undertaken by some of the leading designers in this field. Here, light is an element with the same importance as furniture or layout; it is treated innovatively and imbued with a distinctive personality. In this book, light transcends the simple function of illumination, becoming a tool for emphasizing elements that modify space and turn it into something different by creating an interesting effect or simply a more pleasant atmosphere. This approach leads to homes with their own original identity.

Arturo Álvarez
Bety | 2004
Calor-color

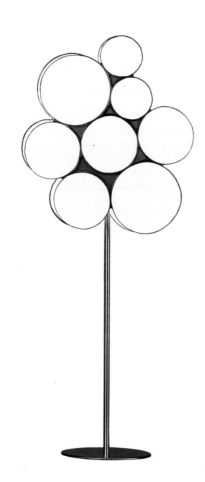

Arturo Álvarez
Gluc | 2004
Calor-color

Arturo Álvarez
Sole colgante | 2004
Calor-color

BEHF Ziviltechnik
Seefels Apartment | 2004
Seefeld, Austria

Conxita Balcells
House Balcells | 2004
Barcelona, Spain

Dive Architects
Clink Street Apartment | 2003
London, UK

Eduard Samsó
Attic in Barcelona | 2004
Barcelona, Spain

Elliot + Associates Architects
North | 2004
Oklahoma City, USA

On the 2nd day of the
new millennium,
our lives were
filled with light.

1-2-2000

Giorgio Gurioli, Gregorio Spini, Marzio Rusconi Clerici
Asana, Sama, Yu | 2003-4
Kundalini

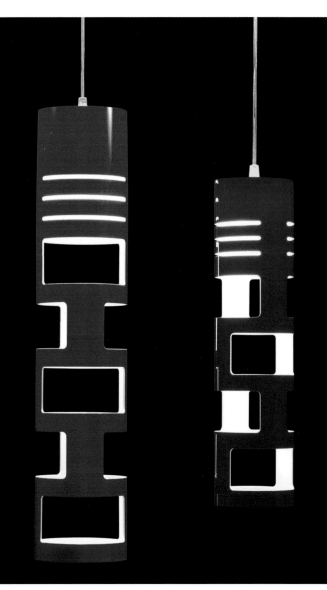

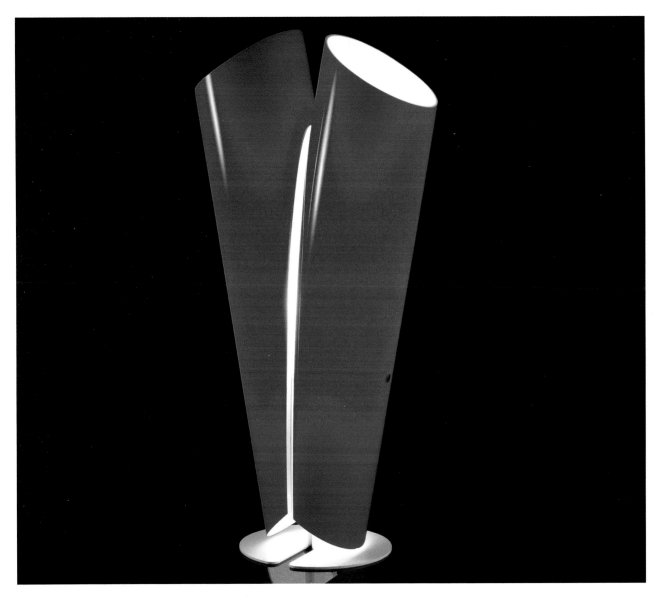

Guillermo Arias
House in Honda | 2003
Honda, Colombia

Gus Wüstemann
Attic in Luzern | 2004
Luzern, Switzerland

Gus Wüstemann
Germania Straße | 2004
Zurich, Switzerland

Harry & Camila 2003
Bolla | 2003
FontanaArte

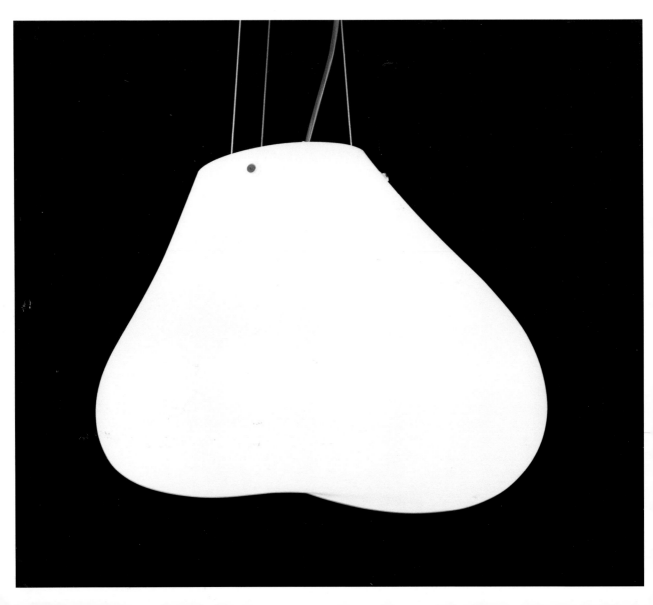

Héctor Fernández
Hlf | 2004
Dab

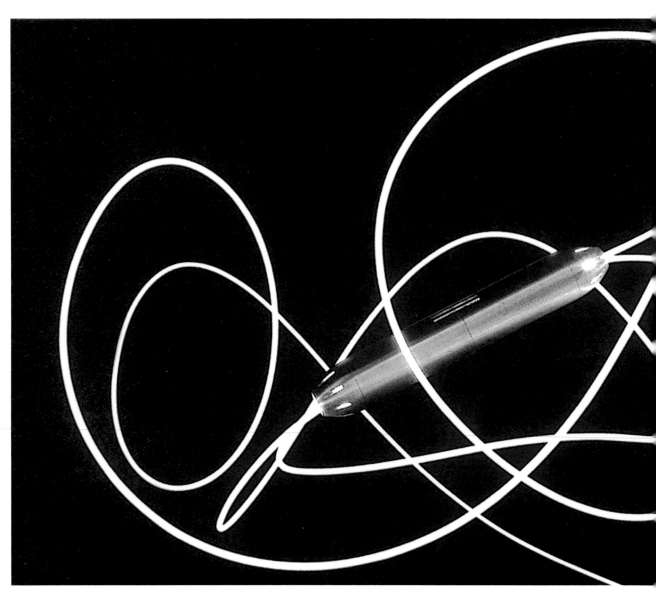

Institut für Raumfreiheit
Loft in Berlin | 2004
Berlin, Germany

Janne Kyttanen
Dahlia | 2004
Freedom of Creation

Jordi Galí
Apartment in Barcelona | 2003
Barcelona, Spain

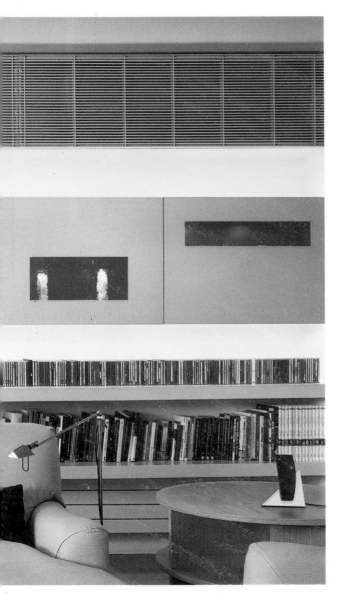

Kazuhiro Yamanaka
Rainyday | 2004
Palluco

Lorena Luccionni
Italian Lighting | 2004
Filottrano, Italy

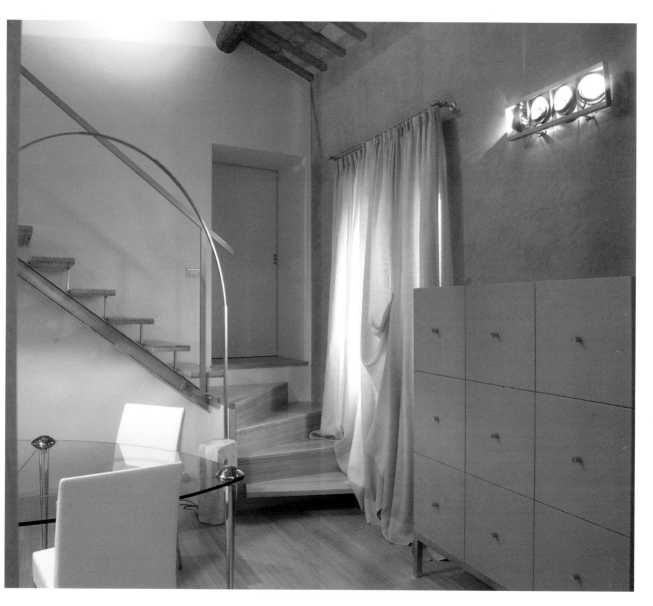

Marc Sadler
Mite & Tite | 2001
Foscarini

Marcel Wanders
Big Shadow | 2004
Cappellini

Marcel Wanders
One Minute Light | 2004
Marcel Wanders

Marcel Wanders
Various | 2003
Mooi

Marco Zanuso jr.
Minimal | 2003
FontanaArte

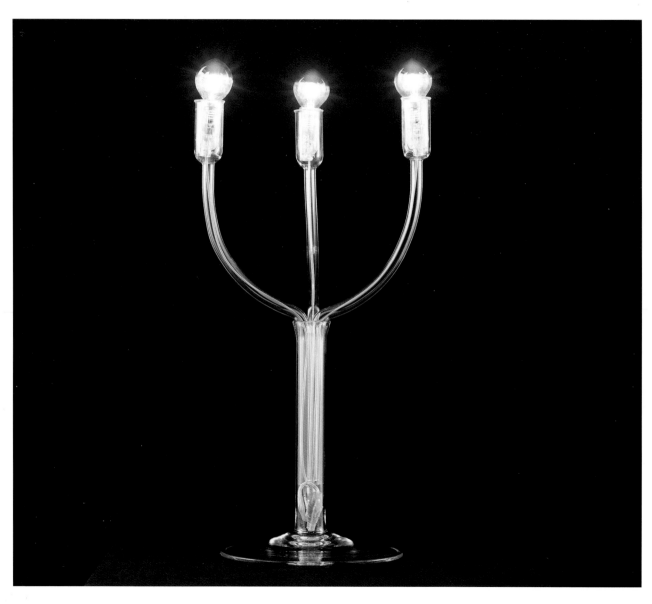

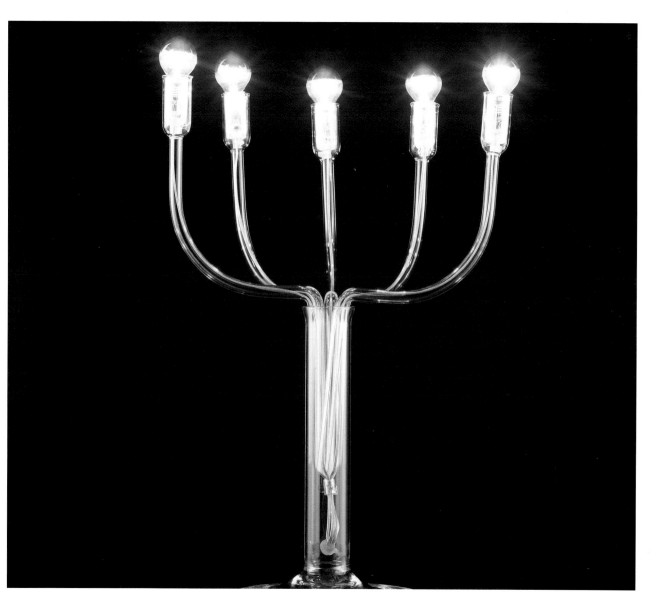

Nancy Robbins
Bluecentre | 2003
Barcelona, Spain

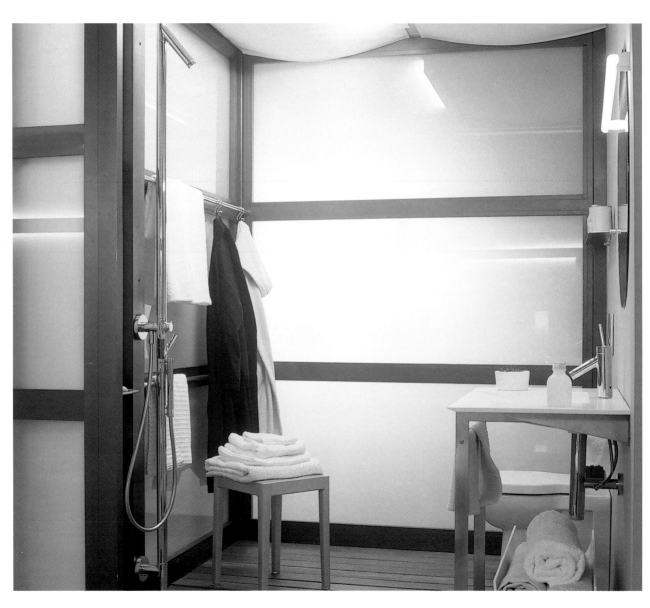

Olga Vidal
Apartment in Maresme | 2004
Barcelona, Spain

Sander Mulder and Dave Keune
Josephine – Marie Lousie | 2004
Büro Vormkrijgers

Simon Conder Associates
Penthouse Flat N1 | 2003
London, UK

Simon Conder Associates
Pinion Barn | 2004
Northhamptonshire, UK

Six Degrees
Australian Flat | 2004
Melbourne, Australia

Studio Kairos
Yet | 2003
Foscarini

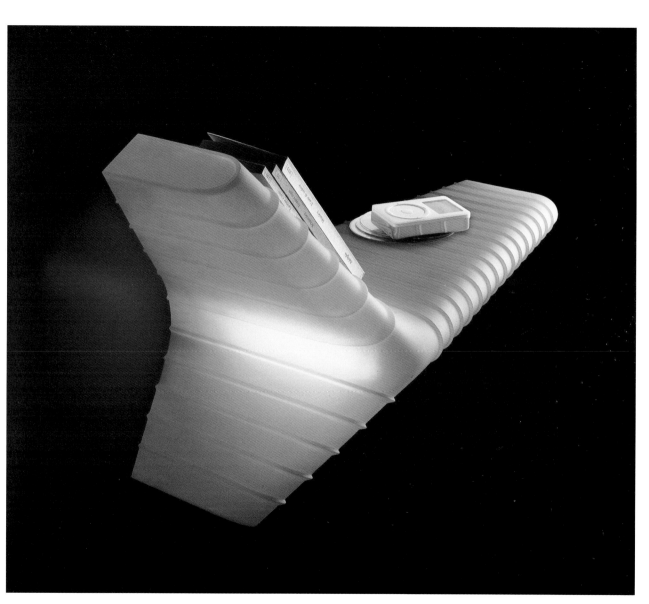

Tonkin Liu
Young House | 2004
London, UK

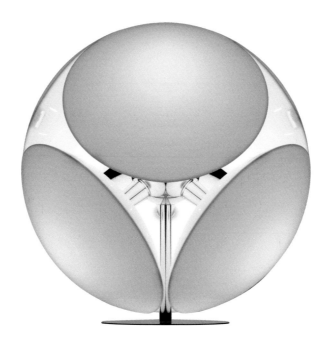

Valerio Bottin
Bubble | 2000
Foscarini

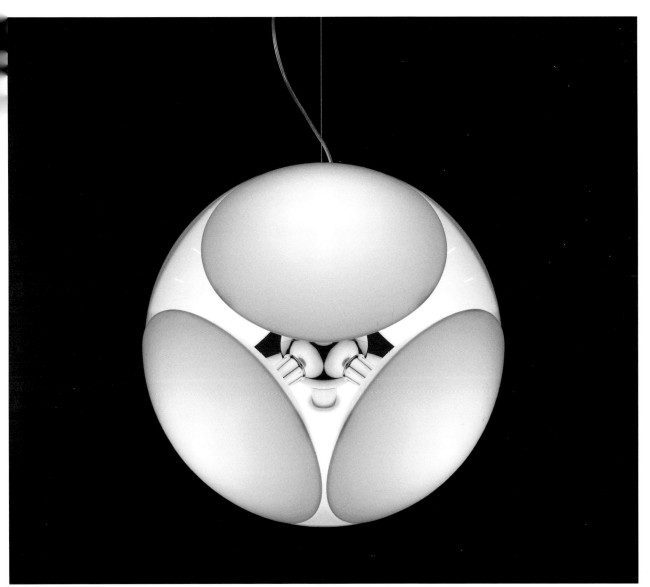

Xavier Claramunt/ADD + Arquitectura
Laiguana | 2003
Barcelona, Spain

51% Studios
Urban Cave | 2004
London, UK

Arturo Álvarez
Calor Color SL
San Miguel de Sarandón, 9
15886 Vedra, A Coruña, Spain
P +34 981 814 600
F +34 981 502 000
www.arturo-alvarez.com
Bety, Gluc, Sole colgante
Photos: © Calor-color

BEHF Ebner Hasenauer Ferenczy ZT GmbH
Kaiserstraße 41, A-1070 Vienna, Austria
P +43 1 524 17 50 12
F +43 1 524 17 50 20
romy.k-debski@behf.at
www.behf.at
Seefels Apartment
Photos: © Rupert Steiner

Conxita Balcells
Casp 35 Entlo.
08010 Barcelona, Spain
c.balcells@terra.es
Balcells House
Photos: © Eugeni Pons

Dive Architects
A009 The Jam Factory
19 Rothsay Street
London SE1 4UF
P +44 (0) 20 7407 0955
mail@divearchitects.com
Clink Street Apartment
Photos: © Jefferson Smith/arcblue.com

Eduard Samsó
Tallers 77 At.
08001 Barcelona, Spain
P +34 933 425 900
Attic in Barcelona
Photos: © Jordi Miralles

Elliot + Associates Architects
35 Harrison Ave.
Oklahoma City, OK 73104, USA
P +1 405 232 9554
F +1 405232 9997
design@e-a-a.com
www.e-a-a.com
North
Photos: © Hedrich Blessing

Giorgio Gurioli
Gregorio Spini
Marzio Rusconi Clerici
Kundalini
Via F. de Sanctis 34
20141 Milan, Italy
P +39 02 8480 0088
F +39 02 8480 0096
www.kundalini.it
info@kundalini.it
Asana, Sama, Yu
Photos: Cesare Medri © Kundalini

Guillermo Arias
Carrera 11 Nº 84-42
Int. 5
Bogotá, Colombia
P +57 1 531 2810
www.octubre.com.co
info@octubre.com.co
Casa en Honda
Photos: © Eduardo Consuegra

Gus Wüstemann Dipl. Arch. ETH SIA
Köchlistrasse 15
8004 Zurich, Switzerland
architects@guswustemann.com
www.guswustemann.com
Attic in Luzern, Germania Straße
Photos: © Reto Guntli/Zapaimages

Harry & Camilla 2003
FontanaArte spa
Alzaia Trieste 49
20094 Milan, Italy
P + 39 02 4512 1
F + 39 02 4512 660
www.fontanaarte.it
Bolla
Photos: © FontanaArte

Héctor Fernández
Dab
Avenida de la Cerdanya, nave 40
Pol. Ind. Pomar de Dalt
08915 Badalona
Barcelona, Spain
P + 34 934 650 818
F + 34 934 654 365
www.dab.es
Hlf
Photos: © Dab

Institut für Raumfreiheit
S 6,22 68161 Mannheim, Germany
P +49 0621 155 932
F +49 0621 151 623
info@raumfreiheit.de
www.raumfreiheit.de
Loft in Berlin
www.berlinerloft.de
Photos: © Werner Hutmacher

Janne Kyttanen
Freedom of Creation
Hobbemakade 85 HS
1017 XP Amsterdam, The Netherlands
P +31(0) 20 427 1575
F +31(0) 20 675 8415
www.freedomofcreation.com
Dahlia
Photos: © FOC

Jordi Galí
Balmes 468
Barcelona, Spain
P + 34 932 115 442
Apartment in Barcelona
Photos: © Jordi Miralles

Kazuhiro Yamanaka
Pallucco Italia Spa
Via Azzi 36
31040 Castagnole di Paese, Italy
P +39 04 2243 8800
F +39 04 2243 8555
infopallucco@palluccobellato.it
Rainyday
Photos: © Palluco

Lorena Luccioni
Via San Lorenzo 40
60024 Filottrano-Ancona, Italy
lorenaluccioni@libero.it
Italian Lighting
Photos: © Alberto Ciampi

Marc Sadler
Foscarini
Via delle Industrie 27
30020 Marcon, Italy
P + 39 (0) 41 595 3811
F + 39 (0) 41 595 3820
www.foscarini.com
Mite &Tite,Yet, Bubble
Photos: © Foscarini

Marcel Wanders
Cappellini
22060 Arosio, Italy
P + 39 (0) 31 759 111
F + 39 (0) 31 763 322
www.cappellini.it
Big Shadow
Photos: © Robbie Kavanagh, Cappellini

Marcel Wanders
Minervum 7003
4817 ZL
PO Box 5703
4801 EC
Breda, The Netherlands
P + 31 (0) 76 578 4444
F + 31 (0) 76 571 0621
One Minute Light
Photos: © Sebastian Westerweel

Marco Zanuso jr.
FontanaArte spa
Alzaia Trieste, 49
20094 Milan, Italy
P + 39 02 45121
F + 39 02 4512 660
www.fontanaarte.it
Minimal
Photos: © FontanaArte

Nancy Robbins
Bluecentre
Photos: © J.L. Hausmann

Olga Vidal Interiorismo
Apartado 512, 08188 Vallromanes, Spain
P/F + 34 935 729 845
Olgavidal91@hotmail.com
Apartment in Maresme
Photos: © J.L. Hausmann

Sander Mulder
Büro Vormkrijgers
Vestdijk 141A
5611 CB Eindhoven, The Netherlands
P +31 (0) 40 213 2547
Josephine – Marie Louise
Photos: Raoul Kramer © Buro Vormkrijgers 2005

Simon Conder Associates
Nile Street Studios
8 Nile Street
London N1 7RF, UK
P +44 (0) 20 7251 2144
F +44 (0) 20 7251 2145
www.simonconder.co.uk
Penthouse Flat N1, Pinion Barn
Photos: © Chris Gascoigne/View

Six Degrees Architecture
100 Adderly St.
West Melbourne
P.O. Box 14003
MCMC Melbourne, Australia 3001
P + 61 3 9321 6565
F + 61 3 9328 4088
www.sixdegrees.com.au
Australian Flat
Photos: © Shania Shegedyn

Studio Kairos
Foscarini
Via delle Industrie 27
30020 Marcon, Italy
P + 39 (0) 41 595 3811
F + 39 (0) 41 595 3820
www.foscarini.com
Yet
Photos: © Foscarini

Tonkin Liu Ltd.
24 Rosebery Avenue
London EC1R 4SX
P +44 020 7837 6255
F +44 020 7837 6277
mail@tonkinliu.co.uk
www.tonkinliu.co.uk
Young House
Photos: © Jefferson Smith/arcblue.com

Valerio Bottin
Foscarini
Via delle Industrie 27
30020 Marcon, Italy
P + 39 (0) 41 595 3811
F + 39 (0) 41 595 3820
www.foscarini.com
Bubble
Photos: © Foscarini

Xavier Claramunt
ADD+Arquitectura
Pellaires 30-38 nave G01
08019 Barcelona, Spain
P +34 933 034 660
Laiguana
Photos: © Joan Mundó
Consultant: Mar Requena (Comunicación)
requena@mrcomunicacion.com

51% Studios Architecture
6th floor, Caxton House, 2 Farringdon Road
London EC1M 3HN, UK
P +44 (0) 8456 123 991
F +44 (0) 8456 123 998
email: hannah@51pct.com
Urban Cave
Photos: © Amos Goldreich

© 2005 daab gmbh
cologne london new york

published and distributed worldwide by
daab gmbh
friesenstr. 50
d - 50670 köln

p +49-221-94 10 740
f +49-221-94 10 741

mail@daab online.de
www.daab-online.de

publisher ralf daab
rdaab@daab-online.de

art director feyyaz
mail@feyyaz.com

editorial project by loft publications
copyright © 2005 loft publications

editor Eva Dallo
layout Ignasi Gracia Blanco
french translation Marion Westerhoff
italian translation Maurizio Silato
german translation Anja Llorella
english translation Matthew Clarke
copy editing Susana González

printed in spain
Anman Gràfiques del Vallès, Spain
www.anman.com

isbn 3-937718-20-6
d.l.: B-24.431-05